Prai

"Zachary Kluckman knows how to animate words. His ability to infuse the surreal into everyday narratives of struggle, joy and desire is impressive to say the least. What a dreamer! I admire his tenacity, vigor and pure unadulterated perseverance. A connoisseur of words, Kluckman knows also how to spin haunting imagery motivated by diction and effortless poetic mechanics. He is a modern confessional storyteller, quintessential dragon slayer and a damn fine poet. Any reader will be thoroughly pleased to stumble upon his work. I'm sure in the hell glad I did."

- Jessica Helen Lopez, Award winning author of *Always Messing with Them Boys*

"Zachary Kluckman's work is a saltline, is a mountain, is a thing to cross only when you have filled yourself to the throat with holy and are ready to walk somewhere. His poems are so much bone and grit and gorgeous open sky, you can't tell when you are crying and when you are laughing because every feeling is alive and raw and open like a nerve. His poems have the mark of what I believe makes a really, really good poet: they tell the truth. Step into the truth with him, you of the holy gut and willing feet. I promise you will not be disappointed. In fact, you might really enjoy the place you have found yourself."

- Melissa May, Author of *Swallow the W i l d*

Praise for *Animals in our Flesh*
Red Mountain Press, 2012

"I like the way the poems grab at two disparate pieces of life and merge them into a beautiful feeling that makes sense on an altered level, a transcendent level, a level that's infused with a broken's heart's love. The words track the relationship between the soul and day to day common life, the words touch the evasive nature of life like fingerprints on flesh, I like the way the poems undulate between mind/heart/soul, blending them into a wholesome evocation of what it his to be alive."

~Jimmy Santiago Baca, Author of *Black Mesa Poems & Singing at the Gates*

Some of it is Muscle

a collection of poetry

Zachary Kluckman

This book is dedicated to my children; Kelsey, Kalvin, Christian and Chance. Every word you speak shatters upon impact with light, becoming one with the universal chorus. Speak freely, speak strength and love easy. You are my anvil.

Table of Contents

Lay me on an anvil, O God
Beat me and hammer me into a crowbar
Let me pry loose old walls
Let me lift and loosen old foundations

- Carl Sandburg

Word Problems

One man, who is an artist, has two dreams and four children. The first dream of the artist is the multiplication of their dreams by an exponential factor of infinity. If each of these children are a brush and the artist has only one canvas, how much paint will he need to pigment a sky big enough for them to believe in? The second dream of the artist is to find a love to replace the one lost in the first part of the equation. His oldest child, the only girl, has three brothers from him. By account of the blood, he is not her father, but he has spent 6,200 days teaching her the words she uses to describe her dreams, which number more than two. Each of her brothers have two dreams of their own, which are a function of living under the normal curve. The mother, who had children with two men, has disappeared into the complicated math of her addiction, the way her skin reacts to liquids. Alcoholism alters the algorithm of her ability to bond with them. The man has been divided by the loss of his wife, leaving him an irrational number. The square root of two. His heart is a train leaving two stations at ninety-five miles an hour. Calculate the force of friction it will take to slow his collision. How fast must he accelerate in another direction to avoid the collision altogether?

InHERitance

The hoarder's closet of stacked keys.
Mementos of bone and convict stamped leather.
Snoopy staring out of Red Baron watches.
Betty Page crouched on black velvet.

The cold whisper of rain soaked freeways.
A long slide down suicide pass in Portland
and the thick brown spiders of Texas.
The eager willow and blood roses.
The long limbs of trees I climbed
with make-shift ropes of water hoses.

Christmas cards from Lone Star prisons
and lemon meringue pie in the windows.
Her quiet depression and moments
of lucid dreaming. On days
when she spoke windows
I could see through her.
The evenings she spent singing to cicadas.

Her favorite song, Rod Stewart
lullabies and late night monster movies.
Rosemary's baby and staring at the world
from a blanket that could never protect me.
I knew she would.

The whiskey scented kitchens
of dirty west Texas and the long lonesome
arroyos of reservations where wind
whispers ghosts in the ditches,
dirt swallows history, touches
your bare feet like hot tears.

The long hair of Samson I found
in a bible she threw in a corner.
The strength of heroes my mother wore

around her eyes in frown lines and furrows.
A knowledge of heaven
I learned from her hands.

Her strength.
Her lungs.
Her unflinching speech.

This weird, broken home
she built, every dirty fingernail.
The muscle of her heart.
The will to dream
out loud, defiantly.

Don Quixote, My Father

He was probably
a better man than I think.

Perhaps a saint
            in sun-burnt armor
when not lost in the lusty, quixotic throes of
almost success that drove him to drink
like a man whose other woman
sends her panties
to arrive in the mail
on Monday mornings;

both threat   and tease.

Perhaps the handfuls
of lysergic acid, LSD
            made a mean sense of
his hopeless desire to be
            somebody's hero;

rescue *her* from a burning building,
save a child from drowning,
eat enough of the sky
to learn the mechanics of wings.

He was probably
preparing a flight path for me,
            in his mind,

a disadvantageous failure to understand that
in battle with windmills
wings could become the enemy.

He was probably
a better man than I think, but

no heroism necessary dad,
just
a better ending
than the one you were writing.

Kissing the Dead on Their Birthdays

Your lips were chapped so badly
by the heat of the fever,
the corners of your mouth bled.

I was afraid to kiss you there.
To taste the thin wine of your death.
Your thick tongue curled back
like a soft bud, unconvinced
of its need for nakedness
under that sun.

We argued to break the silence,
shutter the heart monitor's stammer,
we agreed
you looked like the broken doll
you kept locked in your closet,
unwilling to part with her now.

The last sharp stroke
of the pen that wrote this plot
twist beneath your skin turned
your body inside out, against itself.

We held hands, talked
about anything but the inescapable,
the measure of emptiness that fills
the whorls between our fingerprints,
sounding the body's dull bell
with every touch.

You were still here, hiding
behind the thin cicada skin
you were so anxious to leave hanging
from hospital beds, last breath
caught like cricket song
in the back of your throat.

Two years ago, your body
left you swinging at baseballs in
a dirt lot your mind kept creating from memory.
In the dusty cupboard of your ribs
you found your husband again
and met him for the first time.

One year ago, unconscious, you
smiled at a rocking chair in a room
the sun shone on through
floral print curtains
forty years before.

The only one who
could smell the honeysuckle bloom,
we knew by that smile,
summer was coming back for you.

You would leave with him
the next time he crooned your name
in that cigarette thick,
corn huskers voice.

I couldn't speak the goodbye.
Your body broke when the fever did.
Six months ago.

I've never been good at knowing
what to give at Christmas, on birthdays.
Tonight in the produce section,
I buy a dozen oranges
to hold to my lips.

They remind me of your skin,
the gift I am too late to give.

Nothing Worth Dirtying Your Hands For

When we were five years old
and we needed new shoes for the first day of school
every drop of sweat on our mama's brow
was a silver dollar
she could only afford to spend
because she knew one day
we would have to learn to balance the budget
between our time and our skin
for our children too.

Mama always said
we were the best investment
she ever made.

Children are expensive in more ways
than women can count
by the calluses on their knees.
She gave as good as she could
but when we were twelve years old
and we needed new blue
jeans for school dances,

it was our turn to tend the grass.
We earned our first bruises knocking on doors
until one of the neighbors let us into their yard
where the weeds were as tall as battleships.

We were good soldiers once, weren't we mama?
We pulled acres of weeds until our thumbs bled.
Until green stains and goat-heads made our fingers swell
like ripe grapes on summer vines. We were bursting
with the pride of our early labors, and sore backs
were worth the ten dollars it took for us
to dress up nice for those dates, back when
our hands were still able to pull our earnings from dirt.

Times have changed mama, and our sweat
ain't worth the fraction of a dollar it was in your day.
The jobs have all gone the way of the gray wolf,
and earning a living has become dangerous sport.
They're wrapping hamburgers in college diplomas.
People like us, we've got our backs to the sun
trying to hustle our shadows into giving up quarters.
This ain't the way it was supposed to be mama.

At fifteen I could build an addition on a rich man's home,
sautee a saucepan of shrimp for a perfect ceviche,
and lay a brick walkway from your car to your door
so level you would swear the front yard was crooked.

Last week I asked for work in a kitchen whose sinks
run into drains perfectly dressed in tile neckties
I designed five years ago. When they asked me
for references I showed them my hands. They
complimented me on my work history then turned me away.
My face is a washboard. The shame I carry
won't scrub away clean. What do proud people do
when a lifetime of labor can't earn them a gallon of milk?

I hear they're starting to give up. Starting to wear
their years like heavy coats. There is fear on their faces
and no rebates for the cost of living. When we were children
and we needed new shoes, there was always you
Mama. Always a yard that needed cleaning
or a neighbor's fence to mend. Now we have
children of our own and the unemployment lines
are longer than the checkout lines in grocery stores.

The streets look awful dark when you've got
nowhere to go in the morning and nothing
worth dirtying your hands for.

Whatever You Spend all Your Time Thinking About is God

My bedroom closet was a box.
Eight square feet of faux
wood and plastic
where I hid my books,
buried Playboys under stacks of socks.

At nine years old
a woman's body, full
was sacred geometry.
A holy book full of sin
I was eager to commit

to memory, every curve
an imperfect symmetry.
Goddesses an adolescent boy
might dream of holding.
Every man knows how eagerly
he will pray to the fever
he can touch.

But the idea of God in a book
was a strange fiction written
by the dirty minds of men eager
for reason to disavow skin,
worship something higher.

The instinct to assume prayer posture
a fever of the body harder to explain
than the one to idolize naked women,
seek meaning in sweat and sex,
full of cold promise and meaning
hidden in closets, ashamed
of this thoughtless needing.

Every little boy is torn by the question
of sin, eager to touch God or naked women,
whichever comes under his hand first.

Clown School

I dress and my clothes
smell like last night's dream.

The trees full of eyes,
a thousand black birds
with wings on remote controls.
A million words escape
before my throat can tie the knots
that keep these poems in business.

At times I think the books
are full of lies. A sad saturation
of wet and lonely dreams
the minds of clowns and broken men
have burnt into their pillows,
bound and printed with
their birth certificates.

The post-humous way we speak
their names, a humorous award
for all the things they couldn't say
to another human being
because their eyes were filled
with the lumber of shattered doors.

Scattered, broken toys that lost
their wheels under the storm heels
of tired mothers, the imaginings
of little boys whose only hugs came
from friends they created
when the lights went dark.

Have you heard the one about
little boys who sing behind closet doors
when blue moons and crickets
bulge their pockets with wounded sounds,

when Christmas trees look strong
and tall enough to hold the ornaments
of broken bodies. Their limbs filled
with invisible ropes and children
swinging limp and still.

How about the one where
a nine year old boy held his hand
over his heart like an old man crying
for the no-one-around?

If that old man was your son,
who haunts himself
between the pillows
making breakfast of his body,

eating whatever small scraps of hope
are left scattered in the sheets,
a slow burning candle the trees stare at
through the window, blue boy
in a grown man's body, still
writing poems about the stories
his mind tells him at night,

about broken toys and knotted rope,
would you be jealous of his laughter
knowing he just got the punchline
of the joke?

A Comfortable Pair of Shoes

~for RK

She's a window full of flies.
Wearing a wind-up smile,
the sundial in her eyes
spills shadows down her blouse.

She walks across graveyards
as if bearing her bones to bed.
She's never been easy.

Her hands weren't made for folding,
so her prayers are origami.
Lessons learned hard through repetition.
She sleeps like a vigilante.
Every dream a bounty gathered for money.

Her friends all call her honey
but she'd rather leave the nest building
to the sticky fingers of the men
who've handled her so selfishly.

Her mouth is full of fences.
A row of pickets built around the hollow
home her throat reminds her of
when she cries. The place her daddy
left her and her mommy carved
pumpkins in summer. Left them
on the porches till autumn.
The sweet rotten potential
of all those wasted seeds scares
her more than any twenty dollar ghost
at Halloween ever will.

She's an orphan of regrets.
An apple at the bottom of the drain.

The orange tainted by the worm.
The new dress that only fit at the store.
A pair of shoes stuffed full of cotton,
waiting for someone to spin them
once around the floor, then
return them to the shelf.

Mothers and Daughters

What smiles your slit
wrists made as you imagined
them greeting the neighbors
who found you one morning,
still in your silenced body.

I can't imagine how
you conceived your suicide,
imagined death as parallel to birth.
As if you could walk back
through all of the screaming,
the blood and the breathing
and return to the womb.

There is no mother
waiting at the end of that
long umbilical. She is still here,
struggling to pull you back,
refusing to let go of your hair.
Refusing to let the nurses take
her baby, who isn't crying this time.

I Learn Silence

I learn silence from a woman
who is not afraid to raise her voice.
This makes her silence deeper.

My mother is like the rain
lavishing the trees with kisses,
not to express her love for them
but to make their silence deeper.

I learn to hear the world
with ears that tune to animal sounds,
small and loud, their sounds of wounding
inform my hands of their inherited danger.
I learn to keep my hands in pocket
where the effort of keeping my peace
makes my silence deeper.

From her broken lungs
the sound of whimpers permeate
the unlit corners of our house,
on wheels and cinder blocks, she rocks
and the house moves with her.
I learn to recognize

the changing tones of her
unbearable quiet, the low mewl
of her remembering the loves she lost
or walked away from, the subtle growl
that barely moves her tongue
when she thinks of her brother.
I learn to come undone

in the silence, where it will go
unnoticed by anyone. My cot
on the floor is a harbor where a broken
bodied child crashes like sinking boats

into the swelling storm of his own
unknowing heart. I learn silence
in honor of her crying.

When the world swings
its unjust fist at my missing pieces,
my chest an empty cage filled with
memories of wings and feathered
bodies, my pulse like a song
I want to dance to, full of movements
I can remember, but not commit myself
to learning, these are the only times she sings,
her anger a rising note in pitch black
like birds on telephone lines.

I learn my silence makes her angry.
She does not want this for me.
Does not want my eyes to haunt my face
like blackbirds in countless church windows,
my throat to close over words.
She teaches me to write poetry.

When the cancer comes it attacks her throat.
The soft palate of her mouth removed
to get at the disease. I wonder if they know
what they commit her body to,
a quiet she has spent a lifetime
learning to refuse.

The surgery makes her silence deeper.

When it rains I write a poem
about the white noise of water
pouring over glass and the comfort
it brings me to hear this little noise.
Like static it is silent, but not empty.
When I consider a world

where my mother is gone,
her pained rocking motions
that made our home a lullaby cradle
missing, I learn silence

and the animal sound
my heart makes in its
restless, un-papered cage,
makes my silence deeper.

Cutting the Ties

The dirt faced boy was known to say
that his mother was a blade, his father a crescent moon.
Together they scissored the thread of his fate.

The holes in his jeans gave the blood away.
Homeless as pigeons, the night was his favorite room.
The dirt faced boy was known to say

his mother was a drink the wind left to stir,
his father cut rocks into smaller rocks in the bowl of a spoon.
Together they scissored the thread of his fate.

Each left their impression on the shape of his face.
Howling at bruises the color of shadows left by the moon.
The dirt faced boy was known to say

his mother taught him how to handle a blade,
his father tore his hands open scratching his name on a tomb.
Together they scissored the thread of his fate.

In the hospital his small moon body was saved.
In the dark shadows his voice jumped like a cricket.
Together, the dirt faced boy was known to say
they scissored the thread of his fate.

The Sun is a Bug on the Windshield

The sunset
stays in my windows.
I have trapped it there
with a brush

painting each color's portrait
with the eager optimism
of a sinner
seeking salvation,
with the quick hands
of a junkie,
convinced that rainbows are prisons,

water based prisms
making marionette's of the spectrum.
Colors suspended
by their own lack of faith.

With the skepticism of a father
with no home for his children,
convinced the sky has slit its wrists,
opened the veins in a display
meant for the sun,

a mean ex-lover
whose affairs with the trees
gave birth to the shadows

where my mother was born.
Sculpting mud for a son
she named
carelessly

under the bright,
melancholy suicide of dusk.

Little Red Fire Truck to the Rescue

How many memories begin with little red wagons?

Mine was a fire-truck, but anything on wheels
when you're four is a wagon, so;

how many wagons
pulling how many scrappy little sisters
with sheet metal cuts on their shins
and brown eyes full of *stubborn*?

How many trips to the tree at the end of the block
to fill up on pecans,
carry the rest back in brown
paper grocery sacks?

How many wagons used
to rifle through garbage cans
for old Playboys;
to be sold to the old biker next door
for a pocket full of change

that meant Popeye's spicy chicken,
the world's best buttered biscuits,
a thirty two ounce soda and a hand
full of root beer barrels?

How many people can a fire-truck carry
when it's pulled by a four year old?

It couldn't carry a family.

Or him   my old man,

when they let him out of prison
for one hour that day

so he could
bring it to me
and leave.

Where was my rescue?

Barefoot Bravado

We were eating ourselves in those days.
Angrily tearing off pieces of meat,
masticating the soles of our feet
between gravel teeth and street corners,
making flesh bleed.
When hydrants broke loose, we went dancing.

Maybe it was the heat. All that dancing.
Celebrating sunlight and long days,
we left windows open, let the calendars bleed.
Sweat salting the evenings like meat
we would eat in the morning, sitting on corners
tapping dirty toes and bare feet.

Mailmen would pass within feet
of our homes, dodging large dogs, dancing
away from fireworks burning on corners.
Tree sap on our knees, sticky fingered days.
Cats chasing birds with meat
in their eyes, the leaves burnt and bleeding.

We never questioned cement or the ability to bleed.
Never noticed the calluses on our feet
stricken with seed envy, the taste of fruit's meat.
Desperate to grow and take our shadows dancing,
we counted out the days, waited
under streetlights to watch them passing the corner.

We measured our speed by racing to corners,
nursing our friends when they started to bleed
from exertion, we built bridges by day
that would eventually burn with the friction of our feet.
In the blaze we learned the secret of dancing.
Bright effigies of capable meat.

Like pomegranates, we were more seed than meat.

Thrusting our roots through the cracks on the corners,
holding t-shirts over our heads, flags dancing
before they taught us to bleed.
We weren't used to the weight of these boots on our feet
or their effect on the gravity of a day.

At sunset now we go dancing in our singular meats,
longing for corners and the innocence of days
when our hands held no guns and our friends feet were bare.

The Lions of Dusk

The politicians call it
the international district.
The people who live here
speak its true name with pride.
The war zone, where
the veteran's administration
and hooded, heavy lidded kids
share the drug slingers corner.

The ice cream trucks play
Christmas jingles in the middle
of summer, June dark bodies
like cicadas, the children climb
over fences to chase a white truck
full of paletas. Everyone

holds their breath
until the truck turns the corner.
There is no safety here for children.
Innocence carries no permit.

The slow blue impalas swim
like neon tetras through
the heat haze, windows full of
fever, the anger of poverty
on full display. Survival makes
everyone here a veteran.

The homeless gather
a handful of quarters to rent
space on the mobile homes
of transit lines. The war
rages in silence

until the guns bark
like angry dogs at the neighbors.

Every day here is a fire drill.
The children have *favorite*
places to hide.

There is no protection.
Only the brutal shout of bodies
exploding from bushes.
The little girl's sun dress
blossoms with blood. There will be
flowers on this corner every day
for the rest of the year.

The ice cream man
who drives this route
speeds, afraid of the brown
kids who live in this sector.
He knows survivors sometimes
are the first to turn violent
when threatened.

He is afraid of them for living.
The thin blades of their bodies
lean against his truck, carving
sunlight into ribbons,
feeding their shadows
to the lions of dusk.

Stranger in a Silent Movie

The night might breed streetlights.
Lend cool air a husky perfume.
A mystery best solved by the question.

There's a silence like vinyl
that pops in the groaning of trees on
slender streets, fallen between shadows.

when flies make love to porch lights,
moths fill the air like daytime traffic
but the cars are all still.

Somewhere a stir of canned laughter
crashes through the thin lips of a left
open window, simmers on the sidewalk
like a Sno-cone in Indian Summer.

Gone, it leaves the night more quiet
than before. Lovers roll over in their
leg exposing blankets, resting
from their wrestling.

Down the street, yellow numbers
run in immaculate conception, conceiving
transition, from here to there.

One breath of wind blesses the stillness
like the cinnamon kiss of a woman,
as if the moon were lusting.

Strangers are resting their passion
inside houses, dawning electric morning
of artificial light will lend credence

to their realities.
I wonder if this makes them

more honest than me.

On these empty tarpaulin streets,
the world has grown quiet.
I live with her secret, walk
through her frames like a magnet
in front of the TV, pulling
electrons into synch.

Courting her silence
as she runs through me
like music in a silent movie.

Hollow in the Moon

Sometimes the night is too long. Or the moon too cold in her ignorance of man. Or the birds too still in their night long prayer that the morning will give them a reason to sing.

The blanket sings the skin's whisper with all the intimacy of a lover. The cloth heavy with its softness. A man might lay next to himself on such a night, wrestling with the urge to throw an arm around his shoulder as if offering his coat to a stranger. In this moment between the flight the eye makes on its way to a landscape of dreams and the dawn's eager promise to fill the trees with omens, a soul is like that hollow conch in the bathroom; a place where oceans seem to live hidden, sounding sad crashes on sand. Enough to convince the drifter of sirens and destinies of death and kisses, and what an animal dream it is to inhabit; that place where death sounds sweet if it comes with the hot breath and a lingering lip.

The moon slants through the window and the man, in his bed, carries a fever in his legs; tossing and turning atop the sheets as if his search for a companion required such strenuous effort that even at night he must move. But lonely is the man whose best companion is the moon anyway, regardless of his movement.

Sometimes the wind howls with its stillness. The silence of the unmoving creatures beyond the window a mockery of his fever, a man might lie with a thought like a knife – the crickets will learn his name before another human does. He might begin to listen at the window, straining his ear to catch their symphony of restless legs, to listen for his name repeated in the grass.

The Introvert's Survival Guide

I.

Do not be ashamed of your silence.

Speak only when necessary
and your words will carry
their own weight. This
only makes your voice stronger.

II.

Do not let being alone
make you lonely.
Use the time to unwrap
your middle name like the last box
of dishes from your mothers kitchen.

Learn to love the mirror
for its gentle insistence
that your skin carries light
like a postal worker.
You are here to deliver something.

III.

Treat the word love
like a prayer.

Speak it only when your soul
is shaken by a spirit so strong
you fall to the floor.

Do not expect it to save you.
Love, like prayer, is an act of faith
that makes your body a holy place.

Do not surrender your prayers
to anyone whose hands

are not clean enough to heal.

IV.

When you do choose to speak,
do not whisper like rain.
Claim as much of the air
as your lungs can contain,
scream, like crickets,
like cicadas, covet the moon.
Convince the sky of your claim.

V.

The laughter of children
is the sound the rain is trying to make
when it stands at your door,
wiping its feet, waiting
for invitation,

let it in.
Keep the sky company.

VI.

Scrub the callous from your heart.
All that hard flesh left on the meat
from walking away a hundred,
a thousand times.

Your chest is not filled with feet.
Do not crawl on the floor
looking for love. Stand up.

VII.

When your son says
old people smell like books,
point to the goosebumps.
Tell him

this is the power of his words.
Teach him to understand conversation
as the fine art of carving.

Remind yourself
of this lesson, let silence
be the tool of your creation.

VIII.

A room with six closed doors
is not as inviting as a room with one
that is open.

You are not the only one
who feels lonely. Your heart
is a door. Open it.

Keep the world company.

IX.

Love is not an animal
to be chased by drunken moons.

It is the water where the moon rests,
the hot breath and wild eyes
of something unseen.

Do not be startled
by its movement in the trees.

X.

Never give up on love.
Keep coming back to this.
Not the person who hurt you
but the idea.

Remember that love, like God
is too big to hide forever.

XI.

You will fear your name,
your bottles of leftover rainwater
or your love of cicadas,
have taught the world
to see you as strange.

XII.

Searching the carnival glass
of their eyes, we find the strange beautiful.
Haunting the chapels,
the long halls of their silence
filling their throats with a sound
they have learned to name prayer.
The first to write poems
are always the lonely.

When you feel lonely
enough to write poems,
search your eyes in the mirror
for a sadness that reminds you of home.

Remember every poem you write
is a prayer. You are here
to deliver something.

The word you are looking for is
Hope.

The Lion in G

She leans into Debussy
like a lion,   feasting.

Her fingers on the viola;

wet jaws
working the hamstrings of her hunger.

She's all lean muscle and
long legs straining in her jeans.

The up-tempo piece
stretches her red shirt over
flat belly, breasts thrust upwards
like birds leaving the savannah.

Eyes closed to savor
the delicate pulse in her wrist,
she's leaning back

in her chair, red
plaid pumps kicked back
behind her, with knees bent
at a perfect 90 degrees.

She's turning Debussy in G
into a sensual arrival of moments;
each one coming faster
as the tempo swings up towards
a ceiling vaulted with woodwork

defying the jungle setting;
the salt sweat on her upper lip
        carnivorous.

Long muscle in her arms

wrapping strong fingers around
the thin neck of this viola,

lithe left leg arching foot
back on that four inch heel,
lioness,
at the end of the movement,
licking sweat from her lips

looking oddly shy.

Petting Zoo

When we first spoke of romantic ideas,
those fascinations with razor blade
life lines crossing tightly folded fists,

the secrets you taught your hand
to keep against the bright un-ribboning
of moonlight in midnight parks,

with your feet attempting
to kiss the sky to make the ground
jealous of your weight,

I wonder what you must have seen
to make you, with your blanket of scars
pulled up over your shoulders,

tell me the pain my eyes had mastered
were the deepest pools you had ever seen.

As if this thin attempt to skinny-dip
your way into the artesian well of my workings,
could teach you enough of Braille
to decipher the arctic ridges of my brow.

When you told me your hands
were made of something akin to mercury,
quick to flush with a measure of your uncertainty

I wondered if you would hate me
for attempting to lick
the cyanic corners of your mouth
in an attempt to stop you poisoning yourself
with your tongue.

Somewhere in the unfolding of our secret identities,
revealing more in traded battle scars

than the mere undressing of tender flesh,
we exposed a weakness neither meant to share.

Rattling the cages beneath our breasts
like spider-monkeys at feeding time,
we made a petting zoo of these old wounds

and found a romantic corner of the park
to watch the stars dance like geriatric swingers
full of fond remembrances, pulling the dawn up
around their ankles like bobby socks.

Less Delicate Things

There were less delicate things
in the windows of the glass blowers shop
than there were in your throat
the last time we spoke.

Your voice a high note
in the courtyard of Marriott
when the sax man's baggage broke.
A flute without a reed,
a sound like water slowly
turning a rock.

I knew immediately a boat
had torn loose somewhere from its mooring,
that the tides in your pulse were ebbing,
stranding moonlight on the cold
shore of your wrists.

Somehow the Pacific trade winds
were loose in your chest,
all those little birds,
wings bent by the tempest
scattered and screaming
along the boardwalk of your spine.

Sometimes he stays out
all night, with the boys in the band
and the girls with their tattooed asses
hunt for a good time
and a story to tell over
coffee in the morning.

You haunt the silent phone line,
the shadows of an empty bedroom
like a suitcase full of mimes,
grinning their secret knowledge,

hiding the coins of their eyes

in the corner, by the oven
where you work your magic,
preparing to sacrifice
your reflection in a pot of boiling water.

I try to erect a lighthouse
with the knowledge that even bad
boys become old men, eventually
they learn to appreciate the intimate
intricacies of landing at home.

In the meantime,
there are no anchors to hold
but your own.

Practice Kissing the Rain

Forgive me if I seem out of practice.

In four years I have not kissed
a single lip. Have not spent one moment
lingering over the wet surface, touched
my tongue to thick bottom lip
or bitten it.

I have not felt the faith of face
muscles slipping better judgement loose.
Have not pressed my face into hair
hung heavy with the smell of rain,
hot wax and coconut.

I have not felt the pulse
against my mouth, urging me to
move south. In four years I have not.
Moved south. Or tasted peaches
rolled in warm cinnamon.

I have not kissed you there.
Nor any other woman. For four years
I have kept the same broken promise
you left me with. This amnesiac body
has forgotten how to write invitations.

Has held its breath like a kite
while you tongued rejection letters
to my body on another man's thigh.
For four years the taste of you
has kept my mouth salted.

I have never been kissed
in the rain. Inhaled the thick damp musk
of soil like inner thigh. Warm insistent
breath fresh with a scent like wet grass.

Tonight I forgive my tongue
for the weight of your name.
Four years since I last pressed tongue
to nipple; my mouth to lips swollen with heat.
I forgive myself these necessary
painful absences.

I wash the unspoken loneliness
from my mouth with this rain. Practice
kissing this water in my mouth. Forgive me.
If I seem out of practice, I am sure the sky
will forgive me for swallowing
her thousand small tongues.

A Love Letter Sent to Earth by Meteor

Isn't it true the night
wears her longest coat
when she's with you?
Afraid to expose her full body
before your unbroken stare.

The dark and bloodless moon
of your face is a triumph
the pitiless attach their religions to,
but God help her.
She loves you.

Mother, your children
a brood of war hammers
with thundering hooves. Dark
misbegotten horses, the stars
broken by your kisses.

Was it ageless,
this beauty that turned you?
Countless hands on your body
eager to tame your delicate breasts
and sip at the nectar
of your wetness.

What a bountiless pride
it is that men carry in your presence,
stomping naked through your gardens,
handling your flowers
like weapons.

Are you eager now
to dance them out of your house?
To shoot them with arrows
made of their bones,
plucked from your body?

Perhaps the night
is the only suitor worthy of you.
A lover who sends bouquets
of your own broken body,
returning you
to you.

Conversations with the One I Can't Have

Did it always have to be about
your *particular* orbit? Is your
space so limited one body
can fill it adequately? Is it
so unthinkable to allow me
this one thing?

To let me be the unconscious mind
traipsing through black holes,
discovering the pathways of light?
To let my hands understand

your expanding universe.
Were you afraid of the light
tracing outlines of your body,
swelling the sheets of our bed,
the thick scent of your sex?

Were you afraid I
would smell him on you?
Are you afraid now?
Do the ghosts of *once was*
tangle your hair?

Why do you only fall for men
who will leave you clutching
your chest like a broke strap purse,
hold your ribs closed over the bloodied
bird of your heart, broken,
knowing I was there.

I am here now.

When did you start touching
the walls, the corners of your room
as if they were unfamiliar lovers?

When did we start talking in circles?

Thunder throated stones,
alone with our own gravity,
shall we practice your silence?

This Love Without Words

Your laugh spills across the room when we
dance, the way water falls from rocks in the rain.
This thunderstorm chorus of blood in your wrists
and the swelling skin of your lips.
Your breath a song the wind steals to teach
a man like me to appreciate silence.

There must have been, at least once
another man who loved a woman *like this*.
A woman whose eyes shone fire loud
enough to make her teeth burn in the dark.
Two mad creatures dancing to the sound of rain,
speaking body to body, guttural utterances
and moans, practicing this love
without words.

I want to love you like that. Speak
only a vocabulary of touch, alphabet
of fingertip and animal tongue.
Like the word was never invented.
I want to love you speechless.

The way your eyes love me when
we move together under this moon,
near the long abandoned stones of that
house on the mountain, pressing our lips
like pestle to mortar, crushing
silence into powder.

Love like this must have existed
before the first words ever rose to the lips
of Australopithecus man. Before the
language of our tongues existed, when
instinct ruled the body's movements. When
we would have wrestled like tigers in tall grass,
rough tongued and fierce at our play.

I want to love you primitive.
Rely on the way I rub my head
against your stomach to tell you
how you smell like rain.
How your thighs smell like cinnamon
scented coffee and sun on stones.

Let my hands trace that curve
of lip that hints at a secret.
The swell of you pressed against me,
let the way we lie tangled together
trying to catch stars on
our tongues like fireflies
tell you how much I need you
next to me.

Every word has an origin story.
I want to convince you *this word*
was written in the small
hollow of your throat, waiting
to be discovered by a man who knows
your voice so well he can remember
the first time the confidence rose in it,
the first word you spoke like the origin
of language, the birth of a tongue built
only to shape this word, love.

There is a comfort in silence shared,
a knowledge of the heart without words.
A face you make when you tease, lips
spread in a smile around a tongue as
sweet as nectar in the long necks
of summer honeysuckle.

I want to love you the way a mango
secretly loves the moon.
The way animals love to bite wind.
The way rain clings to stone.

We're still trying
to find a word big enough
for this.

Confessions of the Animal Soul

I.

Sometimes
when you're not looking
I eat without a fork.

Because some inner sense of urgency,
the primacy of the beast
they nicknamed me after in school
compels me to believe
that meat *should* be eaten this way,

with bared teeth, a hint of the fangs
we once carried inside the womb.
When we had gills, a reptilian tendency
to sleep late in the sun.

Some of these habits we never outgrow.
When short days carry long shadows
I still bask in the stretched limb,
the clawed hands of old trees,
long, sibilant S of escaping breath
when the spine turns
just right under the sun.

Some theories suggest that lizards
became birds, others that humans
crawled away with vestigial tails and an urge
to blend into the background when frightened
even by love.

II.

I once attempted making love
to myself by candlelight.

I didn't get lucky
because I had a terrible headache and a fear
of the fire.

III.

Sometimes it is best that we turn ourselves
down because we send such mixed messages
with our morbid desires and curious sensuality

the body is better busied with efforts
to decipher the Morse code of our hands,
tap the inside of our thighs, drum tables,
set signal fires
for lovers we never meant to attract.

IV.

When the symphonies of confession we enact
on our knees begin to subside, the swelling flesh
a pendulum on a downward swing,

I find myself smiling, the same
bared teeth exposed on my face as
the ravenous animal eating those indiscreet
meals with his fingers.

There is something primal
in the way we wet our faces
with the smell of our lovers, something
instinctual

in the way we growl into
each other's face. I can smell it
on your breath, we have not run that far
from the animals in our flesh.

Dirt Pigeons

Love only stands with you until you start hurting.
When the dirt pigeons prowl the bones, scissoring tendons,
the thunder dives in your wrist. Crimson tides ebbing,
the love you count permanent is only a shadow

where the dirt pigeons prowl the bones, scissoring tendons.
Your faith is a square stone stalking the horizon.
The love you count permanent is only a shadow.
You fear the living are cardboard cut to fit parade routes.

Your faith a square stone stalking the horizon,
the lie is not your solitude, but your comfort with quiet.
You fear the living are cardboard cut to fit parade routes. Prayer
is either superstition or the way your body mourns.

The lie is not your solitude, but your comfort with quiet.
The thunder dives in your wrist, crimson tides ebbing.
Prayer is either superstition or the way your body mourns.
Love only stands with you until you start hurting.

Single Parents

~Co-authored by Jessica Helen Lopez for the 2013 Albuquerque national poetry slam team

You are not the Disneyland parent.
You count pennies in brown paper rolls,
imagine your children chewing
their own tongues for moisture
when the water bill isn't paid.

You wash dirty jeans in the bathtub
because there aren't enough quarters
for the machine and the kitchen sink
is full of things thawing for dinner.

Single parents spend a lot of time in the kitchen.
This is where we feed them
something more than excuses.

You will never take another
uninterrupted shit, or know
a whole night's worth of sleep.

You are always first to wake,
last to eat,
primary caregiver,
fighter for child support,
supplier of Band-aids
tit and talon,
fierce as lioness.

Trim the bangs,
trim fingernails,
make breakfast,
wash dishes,
dishes, dishes,
dishes.

You will spend a *lot* of time
in your kitchen.

Raising and rearing
the split cells of your self,
rising every day
with the breath of their breath
in your lungs.

The only one to attend
parent teacher conferences,
you navigate city transit systems
with your kids like stray current
crossing the wires.

Four hour bus rides
to school, the dentist
and straight on to the horizon.

You will never buy brand name anything.
Buy enough groceries for two homes
so your children can eat while your ex
sleeps it off again.

You grin and swallow your words
when the kids thank them
for the new shoes you bought,

because single parents can only afford
the luxury of standing on moral principle,
when they are not already standing
on tired feet in front of school principals.

You will wear the wood thin carrying
the children to bed.
When everyone else has
a new dream tucked under their pillow,
\

you sleep
alone.

Because single parents don't have sex.
Often enough.

When you do
it's fast and dirty.
Bathroom door closed,
bent over hamper
hand over mouth,
so your sounds of pleasure
won't scare the children
like dropped glasses
in the kitchen.

Single parent means
you don't cry in front of your children.
Or you cry an awful lot in front of your children.
Like the day I filed for custody
and my child's face
was a mask of questions I couldn't answer.

My breastbone dismantled
under the weight of my losses,
I couldn't rise from my bed for days.
My daughter; my fear that I just may fail
at motherhood.

That night I strangled screams
in knotted up pillows, shaped a dream to fit
my fear of joining the homeless.

You will give up.

At three in the morning when candles
hold their breath until blue faced and tepid,
waiting for answers to rain down your windows

you *will* give up.

When your heart strings are broken like pawn shop violins,
your children offer the easy grace of forgiveness.
You must tend to the pattern of sleep,
that cadence of breathing.
It's the littlest things that describe
love's labor as softness.

Single parenting is a torch-song,
a love letter from the utero.
A sacred heart cracked open,
and no, you never thought
it would be like this.

But, here it is,
a tight-fist of love.

In the morning you will uncurl your body
and hold your child one minute longer
as the day breaks
in all the ways
you won't.

How to Hang a Picture

It's all about the nail.
Too thin and the weight of attached
memory will shatter on tile
like the silence that fills
your house with heartbeats.

Too thick and the stubborn wood
that supports your walls
will resist the point,
the intrusion of joining.

Too short, like the moment
your photo captures and even
thick tempered metal will not hold.

You must find a nail
as long as your tongue,
measured from jaw to end of nose.

Prefer one orange with rust,
recently removed from other walls,
tarnished with the memory of other
pictures, proven strong enough
already to refuse the bend
or saw of wire.

To penetrate soft plaster,
your thumbnail makes an adequate drill,
torn from hand after
badly timed hammer falls.

It is best to set the nail
with single strike, to avoid
the crack that webs the gypsum.

Hang your memories
at the level of your eyes.
Do not let temptation to forget
drive you to hang these photos
above the knees where bruises
grow as purple as your thumb,
hammer struck numb.

The past should not force you
into prayer posture. Remember
the room will now be initiated
to the secrets of all
you have chosen to allow
of memory, only your hands
will know what photos
you have selected to haunt
their frames unhung and quiet,
whispering behind boxes.

Forgiveness is a Small Boat

You were *almost*
A silk-worms' favorite leaf
once

Almost
delicate.

Slender wristed
as the throat of those orchids
we talked about planting at Christmas,

you could never catch rain.
I knew we were doomed.

The heart is a drunken architect
full of blue prints and sky scrapers.
No one understands his designs.

When you danced yourself naked
through the tawdry offices of my mind,
upsetting the furniture,
teaching the windows to sing
like wine glasses at Hollywood weddings,

you were the rain.

All throaty laughs and light touches.
You were the leaves dancing over
concrete in autumn,
red eyed and wicked.

Waiting for someone to jump in.

I was a leaf gatherer,
chasing these widows of spring.
Pressing lovers into bed sheets
the way maple folds against the spine
of old journals,
biting at bindings.

A canvas topped Samson loose
in the city, assaulting bookstores,
setting poems free from the backs of old books.

You were *almost* delicate.
I more rebellious,
a bee in the window
your eyes could never quite close.

Somewhere in Albuquerque
there is a church that remembers
the prayers of our feet.

Inside that church there is a closet
where we *almost* committed a sin,
a broom that has seen you naked
and a flowerbed where I buried our vows
w you weren't looking.

As this earth is my witness,

you were the rain.

I have stood naked inside of you,
surprised
at your violence.

The Night the Rainbirds Sang

I collected the water.
Rain baskets, my hands.
The webbed flesh a promise.
So busy with gathering
what you needed, I missed
all signs of you leaving.

The slack shouldered taxi cabs
with their yellow fever,
parked outside for a week.

The wet feet of passing cats.
Some ancient instinct leading them
to step around puddles as if
not already wet, you
admired their grace in avoiding
uncomfortable situations.

Umbrellas dancing over sidewalks.
Spinning red penumbras. Colored
silk between trees. A lamppost
choreography of leaving.

Caterpillars exploding
from the shaggy heads
of water heavy elms, students
running from classrooms.
The rain is never empty.

An ocean of flashing bodies,
silver skinned by wet streetlights,
a high tide of specters on sidewalks.
Rain singing like birds in the culverts,
teaching concrete to sing.

Somewhere in that storm,
I spilled the water. One of these
wet ghosts crossing the street
is you. Sometimes I look.

The Sky is Black with Pearly Birds

Your passing will be marked
with one long shadow
          under a tree grown thin with winter.

One gaunt finger of
wind burnt bark and
fallen leaf
          clawing fleshy sky.
On the day
you are proclaimed to earth,

given stone to stand your ghost upon

with whatever small comfort
one can find in words spoken over them,

you will hear
the pearly birds of shadow
slap their wings against the
          startled sky.
A sound reminiscent of clapping,

a release of starlings from the trees
as if celebrating
your marriage to the earth.

I wait for you,   my old friend
to relive the nights you spent
with my own black pearl
          secreted in your hands,
to consummate with you
this long ceremony of earth and time,

beating sand
          and baring bones.

Stamped Metal Flowers

We folded our bodies
into displays of affection.
Aluminum foil puppets wrapped
around coat hangers.

Marionette movements
informed with the alchemy of sex,
we staged our marriage.
Made stamped metal plates of our fingerprints
so we would never forget to pray on Sundays
and mention the others name.

When I bled
from the wedding chalice
that broke in the dishwater,
you collected my fluids,
bright copper coins, ran them through
your fingers like a tourist attraction
then offered them back
as a souvenir of your visit.

We made a dark art of our love,
crafted masks so frightful even
the night could not recognize us. The *santos*
 in the candles prayed every night for our souls.
 When we burned our bed
The sweet blood musk and sweat
offered a softness we never allowed,
or couldn't prevent.
We gave ourselves over until spent.
Our fingernails glowed with remembrance of
touch like *luminarias* at Christmas.

We were sheet metal flowers.
Marigolds with a long memory of pain.

Gratitude

Thankful for the hard callus on knuckles
that hides me from you. Thankful for the twist
in the wrist that means the scars
wrap around, bleeding into life lines.

Thankful for the ribbon of cum
that slid down my thigh, a wide warm
welcome for the small death that follows.
Thankful for the way you hunt my scent among pillows.

Thankful for the aspirin of your smile,
for your teeth like bright pills crushed into my mouth
when we kiss. Thankful for the scalpel
of your lips, for your surgical bed.

Thankful for the folding chair of your spine,
for the horizon I watch rising and falling
under the influence of your breath.
Thankful for the cumulous in your lungs.

Thankful for the silver clouds you paint
with the stolen lumens of light bulbs,
for the reflective surface of mirrors you hang
in the closets, reminding me not to hide there.

Thankful for the sarcastic love we make
over bed springs with their own sordid opinions
of the weight of our bodies and the ways
we wrap our tongues into coils.

Thankful for the indigenous skin
we find ourselves invading every morning.
Sweating trade made with our hands
pressed into prayer patterns and palm offerings.

Thankful for the bathtub in the swelter,

the lime colored tiles on the ceiling,
the water marked rust colored in the sink.
Thankful for the drains in your palms,

for their power to heal the stigmata
of blood that flowers in my hands
when I attempt to plant seeds of forgiveness
in the broken earth of my body.

Thankful for the delicate yellow flower
that stepped under my foot yesterday,
indignant at my attempts to straighten her folds,
to let my clumsy hands practice medicine

when it was my touch that broke her.
Thankful for this reminder that patience
is a means of deception, a lie told in the long hours
of waiting in white halls for doctors,

waiting for physician time to make house calls.
Thankful for the children who answer
their mother's phones, for the kindness of receptions
given when the terms of surrender are met.

For the moment when the heart
stops polishing it weapons and the closets
burst like ripe fruit, while the mirrors
explode into wind chimes, thankful

for a history of mixed messages,
for the witness protection
offered by sharing our bodies. For the shivering
animal our time has become.

Thankful that our decisions
shared their small triumphs with us,
for the ridiculous clown that is love,
for the small surface of your tongue,

where I learned to count my blessings
in the small disappearing of hurts,
in eight eyes that remind me of yours,
thankful for the grace in the long curves

of the screws that we turn with our eyes
while we sleep.

Collecting Sunburns & Cigarettes

I wonder how many memories we missed
collecting sunburns and cigarettes
in the window of that old two story
red brick faced apartment,
staring out towards the sea
as if we could smell it
500 miles away
if we waited long enough
for a breeze with nothing better to do.

Remember how the window sill stuck
in the frame? How the flies
buzzed, trapped between glass
like *i love you*
in the back of your throat?

You folded your long
arms out over the edge, leaned
into the sun while it blushed
the loose skin over your breasts,
stretched by years of gravity
and goosefleshed children.

How many times did we
consider the fire escape
when the landlord came knocking,
calling for rent?

We should have done it.
Should have taken whatever money
we had crushed in our pockets, grabbed
keys from coffee table and bolted
over and out the window like spiders
running from thunder.

We should have left notes

written in butter smeared on linoleum floor,
proof of our escape waiting
for the debt collectors
to trip over in the kitchen.
We should have run.

Should have fled for that sea
we kept imagining, that sand
under our feet as we spilled like loose change,
tumbled laughter across whatever
beaches we could conjure, whatever
towns we could reach
on fifty bucks worth of gas
and pastrami.

Dark horses flashing through trees
like this good memory of the escapes
we should have made. You
must have dreamt often of running.

Maybe I would have been
a better husband to help you escape, but
I loved our shitty little apartment
with it's leaky faucets and the ghost
I'm convinced we out-haunted,

for that sticky window that brought
sunset to our table, where we
worried the future in tight little fists
the first time the doctor told us you were pregnant.

Where Easter parades and gay pride
demonstrations marched beneath our windows,
the park across the street
gave us young lovers on benches.
The rent was too expensive,

but that's not why you ran

out on us with your skirt lifted,
your shattered glass slippers
cutting your feet into ribbons.
There were still some fairy tales
you needed to believe in.

I'm sorry I never helped you escape.

That old window has our memory
carved in its frame. The kids and I drive by
in summer to watch us
there in the glass, catching
sunburns and cigarettes like fireflies.

I wonder if the place is still haunted.

Autophobia

There must be, within me
some fear you could call illogical,
but some days it feels like a lifetime
wearing scars for eyes

has left me little fear of anything,
except everything.
Spiders maybe.

The way they crawled across my body
at the hands of my uncle,
made *six years old*
feel like a treasure map.

His hands loved to travel.

Discovering shame
would leave anyone afraid
of their phantom legs.

This quickening silence I am afraid of.
Loneliness.
Isolation.
A life without meaning.

Isn't everyone afraid of learning
the light they bring to the table
burns out with their leaving?

This life I've spent hiding
under herb gardens,
huddled under window boxes,
keeps me too busy bookkeeping,
tracking the numbers of bridges
I've left burning behind,
to develop a phobia of anything

as small as death or crowds.

Both, after all, end with me
pressed up against walls,
looking for some hole to fill.
Confessing to shadows as they
crawl into my lap with the setting sun,
petty crimes committed by kids.

Regrets I stack in the closet
behind the water heater.
The cocaine cracked nose
worn thin with use, the blood
that reminded me of family,
the father I could never be,
shoplifting food for my daughter.

The son my mother needed.
A wife I gave a hundred orgasms to
in place of a companion.

The weakness I bring to my failing.
The rolling island in the kitchen
where the knives are kept hidden.

This shortness of breath.
This breath.

This catalogue of breaths taken
defined by the sound a throat makes,
as close as thunder in my chest.

This fear, defined by the movements
of hiding I make in my waking.

This struggle with darkness,
an autophobic response to the morning.

This promise I make to stop hiding.
This promise. This life.
This living.

Let the Past Lie

The clock is not aware of its own nudity.
This is why they never blush when
racing face first towards dawn.
Somewhere between the bathroom
and breakfast we find the time to be
surprised at how much of it we never got back.

These déjà vu trysts are the only visits
we receive from the children of all those hours
we impregnated with forgetfulness. Old
men, grown thin in hair and hours.
Looking at our hands as if they
were the protagonists in a story we were sure
we were there to witness
but forgot during hangovers.

Old friends, these hands
with a knowledge we once shared
with a nod. The thumbs especially wicked.

Odd, how vivid the memories of them are.
The hitched rides to artesian wells
for mushroom picking and fumbling
at bras. Still unmastered, those bras.

The curve of a cheekbone beneath
them, on days that demanded more couch time
with a woman whose arms were
every excuse for gold as the color of suntans.
We danced to scratched records as if
passing the seconds in a meteor shower
the Pleaides would give its left nebulae to produce.

A delicate pattern of water on concrete.
Time, like the droplets we waste watering
the weeds, is predisposed to scattering. The

clock's effort to put on its best face is wasted
by our insistence on covering each moment's
nakedness with memory.

Blue Note for Chance

Everything
I have ever believed
lives in the body of a seven-year-old boy.

I know he's not ready
for this responsibility.
Neither am I.

But your leaving
left us
no choice.

I remember the day he was born.
Our little boy,
blue.

Umbilical wrapped around his throat.

Me, holding you.
Pressing my hands against
the small of your back
to relieve the pressure
from your spine.

Blood burst across the gurney,
an offering to some thirsty god.

The nurses.
      All their running.
White shoes thundering in that room.

I remember you
watching me
holding him.
Returning to color
after they cut the umbilical loose.

You were holding him *too tightly* then.
Your body
refusing to let go of him.

God, I loved you then.

Beautiful, blonde Atlas
ready to shrug.

The whole world
weighed less than eight pounds once.

Now our son
asks me to tell him stories
so he can sleep while you're away.
I tell him how
the red-breasted Robin
wore the wrong shirt to work.

What perfect mistakes we make
when we forget our own natures.

I tell him how, sometimes
the tornado seems to swallow
the whole sky but the sun
closes its eyes. When those storms
pass, all the birds return
wearing the right shirts.

Innocence and faith
never wore such beautiful skin.

I wish you could see him.

Seven years old, he makes me feel
weak
and stupid.

When we drive-thru for fast food,
I reach to roll the windows up,
turn the stereo on.
He laughs and says
Dad, I can still hear the birds beat-boxing.

When I ask about dreams he says
Dad, I had a dream the trees were dancing
and I was a leaf.

I wonder why we listen to music
when we can learn such easy lessons
from laughing. Why
we complicate dreams with need
for interpretation. I wonder
how he knows so much
when I can barely put the words
together to tell you

that I miss you.

That I love you.

That we'll be alright

without you.

Love Letters from a Laundromat

Soap and shit smell sweet together.
A perfume the blue vested woman
chases from her nostrils with bourbon
and smoke when she gets home.

The Laundromat filled with brown
skinned boys laughing at little girls,
crawling on top of belching machines,
rag doll legs stuck over their lips,
triple load monsters
with their tongues out in the heat.

The sweat pools in cracked lips.
An old woman's face
refracts light, soap cakes
her knuckles as she folds fists
in the tight squares of cloth,
a perfect crease in every blouse.
A move she has practiced for thirty years.

Arcade games as ancient
as the droppings mice play kickball with,
skittering across floors, corner
to corner. Children
with elbows dry as the dirt
in blue pockets, white tooth
smiles, hammer the knobs and punch
quarters into slots.

Quiet as moonlight on dirty wash water,
I listen as their jeans wear down
to bare thread. This is our life.

Later, I will stitch his threads
into something resembling
the shape of a knee so he can wrestle

again with the trees,
Quixote threatening grass
with the weight of his body.

My son at five is Titan
in a toddler's body. Underwear
so small it hangs like a kite,
he climbs under rubber topped tables,
chasing the smile a young girl carries
like a bright penny from her mother.

Dryer sheets cling to
my fingers the way his hands,
as small as oranges, still do.
Little boys are fish boned creatures,
all eyes, teeth and mouth.

This is us, Saturday night.
Folding underwear, creased
sleeves and hanger bent jeans.
He asks for her name while I fold.
She wets his cheek with a kiss.

His eyes shine like light
was just pulled fresh from the machine.

An Easter Letter from the Detention Center

On the margin, with twin clouds
for cheekbones, a rainbow
is scrawled with such purpose
of color I can picture her
smile as tight as a garrote.

Desperate little girl in a four by six cell.
Fumbling for a sense of innocence
in the shape of hearts she has drawn,
erased and drawn again.

Her hands have forgotten
the ease they once found
fluid as blue ink, writing
to inform me the judge
has ordered her to ninety days
in residential treatment.

Happy Easter Daddy. Tell the boys
how much I love them. I'm sorry
I'll miss the little man's birthday.

My daughter at fifteen is water.

On paper borders, she scrawls
her initials, as if she could stand
with both feet on this one small
possession inside her cell,
irrigating her claim
with the sweat of her
efforts to smile, crafting
words to a father
she's afraid has forgotten

how brave little girls
can be when they're smiling.

How easily their bright-eyed shine
can be coaxed to the surface
by men who remember their promise.

I don't wear as much make-up now.
Dad. I've put on a few pounds. I'm almost
a trustee. In two days they will let me
work in the kitchen.

Outside, the sun
flirts dangerously with thick charcoal
smoke. Hickory and laughter
bubble over chicken. Jump-ropes
hang in the air like wind-chimes.

Training Day

~for Kalvin

He says he could take me in a fight.
This is not a challenge to my skill with knuckle bone
and kneecap. It is his statement of time. Acknowledgement
that the sun has passed over his shoulder often enough.
That his shadow is ready to challenge the ground
for permanent possession. My teeth respond to him

rolling their thin sleeves up, exposed
as the white elbow bone his skinny arms
wave like an ID card. Old as he may feel,
the inflection of our wrists punch commas
in the language of our sweat.
His mouth is full of men's teeth,
but he is afraid for his strength. Afraid
his body is limited to awkward imitations.

Fifteen years of soccer fields and sweat
have packed his chest with batteries, igniting chemical
fire in his blood. His biceps are thick, boiled rope.
His body is all nerve ending and balls. His shirtless
chest stretches sacred supple, lean muscle under
forty pounds of hard steel. Untouchable.

Five sets of curls, fifteen reps with barbells
next to the sofa. This couch that has seen us cry
when the fox and the hound were parted, each
gone to his role in a world where strength is weightless
in the face of expectations. This room where he
swallows pills for a depression his body curls
around on days when the weight is too much.

It will not be long before his boast becomes
a fact we will have to accept on faith. He will learn
soon enough that thick arms and six pack abs are an armor

as thin as umbrellas. That the body is a tourist attraction.
A curious circus of shapely performers entertaining
the crowds while the heart learns to endure. That these
two hour prayers to a manhood he perceives
in gravity and iron must be matched

by faith in the patience that time demands.
Our bodies are built by tearing the muscles. We lift
heavier and heavier weights until the joints fill
with lactic acid and burn. Set fires in sinew and bone,
purify the soft tissue. He is one hundred twenty pounds
of lean muscle. I am two forty.
Some of it is muscle.

We flex, stretch and cool down. His smile
is crooked with the arrogance of youth. My son,
with his beautiful strength. This is how
we acknowledge the heart.
As strength. As work. As muscle.

Storm Warning

The rain makes stringed instruments of
our hair, beads on kitchen curtains, love
knots for our children to climb, losing
themselves in our tangles.

Our search for their missing smiles is
the meaning we assign to water, to blue.
The reason we consider the sky broken,
peel the horizon bloody from streetlights.
Paint the curbs with our feet, find harmony
with the rain by matching our hips
to bare roots, slip loose from dirt.
Move

past trees smoky and bored
as the musician outside a club
where the old men dance only to classics,
like love, gone missing for cigarettes.
An angel divorcing her children. A man
in a city where other men name their adultery
foreplay,

blame bored wives sitting in windows
making a strong tea of patience, heart
a small fly drowned wingless and broken.

We blame the rain for the weight of the sky
as easily as we blame each other's bodies
for silence, as dull toothed and pointless
as blaming you for owning a soul too old
to remember naming the sky hydrant,

the stars streetlights, gathering
their numbers near water, running
up and down basketball courts
in their sandals

---

move

past memories of childhood to the rain
you remember by its initials, carved
in the dirt outside our door. Count the pearls
of water spilled down our daughter's throat,
a broken necklace the sun borrows to stain glass
her reflection. Count the number of freckles
on our son's shoulders, divide by four
because math makes more sense than love.
Move

like October leaves chasing the wind.
When you left, the only meaning I could speak
to your absence was the wind listening
to a bell ring and chasing curious after,
eager to swallow the sound so it can
impress the trees with a song it's just learned,
like a child it is not her nature to stand still.
Move

through rain, seeking whatever fever
of jazz, gin or fear it is you've come
so close to the earth to learn, lean close
to the windows, listen.

When a child tries to find
his absent mother in his father's arms,
thinks she is waiting somewhere inside him,
like a prize they can win if they pray
or bite hard enough, all a man can do

is hold them to his chest, threaten the thunder
to stop scaring his children, whisper.
Tell them how she smelled like water,
how her breath was the window rain looked through.

How she taught him the classics

like love, like absence, like children
waiting for their father to stop
watching the rain carry their home
down a hill.

A Poem for the End of the World

~In the wake of the Sandy Hooks Elementary School shooting

I.

The end of the world came
and went. Again. Another candle lit
in the funeral parlor for the dearly departed
who did not have the decency
to send a note that he wouldn't be coming

because five days ago someone
murdered the children. There was no one left
for the world to widow. No one
who did not feel it had
already ended.

II.

There was never going to be enough time.

Our bodies were meant to be yo-yos.
Arms and legs swinging wild in whatever
small space we were given to fit
inside this world.

We were meant to collide. To crash into
each other's bodies like the sea, crushing rocks
with a husky voice, a chorus of waves
laughing. Blue eyes

in wild round faces. Our legs scissoring
the air as we flew. The swing-sets creaking
like old mama's teeth. We were meant
to be young forever.

There was never going to be
enough time to play.

III.

Because if the world ended tomorrow
as predicted, I would not have told you the truth.
That I have always loved you. How I imagine
our old age as a sunset we add paint to
each day. Even if I am the only one who knows
there are brushes in our hands.

I would not have spent enough time
with my children. Would not have chased
them up deer trails to the crest of
the Sandia mountains, watched them
as they stuck their tongues out like animals,
trying to catch a mouthful of water
from the sky.

I would not have forgiven you, mother
for your fears. You father, for your disease.
Would not have forgiven you, my sister
for leaving. Or you, poet, for believing
it would ever be easy.

IV.

Five days ago someone murdered
the children. Billions of children ago,
God set off an explosion to fill the universe
with light and the sound of creation. That sound
has filled our children's ears with a song
they have no name for, so they fashion themselves
artists and draw pictures in crayon.

These are the artists who will remember
our songs. Remember what all of this sounded like.

What we sounded like, worrying ourselves sick
with the end of the world.

As if it did not end
every time one of them
was taken.

A Walk in the Park

He will run up
in baggy pants, boxer shorts
the same shade of indignant
as the bandana around his head.
Hands behind his back
like a priest after confession,
worrying salvation
may come a little late,

but this boy's crucifix
is triggered, cocked in his fist.
He is fifteen years old, at most.
Moustache a small slouch across his chin,
thin eyes full of the righteous
religious fanatics hide
their uncertainty with.

He owns this side of the street,
at least in the moist, dark parts
where his thoughts echo with visions
of a bad reputation, street credit.
He is someone's brother.
Someone I probably won't remember.

But he has heard stories of me,
stories rubbed raw from retelling,
until his eyes shine with them
like obsidian rosary beads.
I will tell him those stories
are exaggerated, rumors spread
until they grew too big
to fit me anymore.

I will tell him I understand.
I drew the same angry breath,
the same moon spoke to my heart

like a mad girlfriend in a streetfight.
I will tell him the truth.

The streets don't give one good
goddamn who you are.
You can't trade street credit for bread.

I will tell him when I
wore his shoes with pride
and dirty shoelaces,
I was a liar too.

All I ever wanted
was to be someone's father.

That when I got older,
I had those children, and one day
maybe he will too.
Maybe he'll have a daughter.

One day he will walk her
to the park, trusting the
safety of sunlight,
until some kid with ideas
of vengeance for crimes committed
in the tempest of youth
will come up to him
the way he does now.

How will you feel
when this angry kid pulls
his weapon and points it at you
in front of her,
or at her.

You can't protect her
because the orgasms of violence
shuddering down his spine

tell him that blood
will make him a man.

Go home.
Trade your gun for a poem.
Learn the names of every saint.

Pray the past will leave you alone.

Cars Become Metronomes in the Rain

The streets are singing,
           or maybe

that's just the rain
playing the curb's black and white
keys. Ghetto tract symphony.

Listen, damn it,

listen.

Wind strumming sheets of water
running into gutters, wet words
rushing up from the ground,

or maybe

that's just the homeless man,
praying.

Red flannel jacket,
torn hemlines
a feathered bursting,
untucked corners hanging
over dirty leather belt,
his fingernails,

his fingernails…

A delicate thunder of water
meeting thin sheet metal
hoods, black bars humming
Gregorian chants.

Porch awnings,
car roofs, salt rusted hoods.
Traffic an Italian tenor toning
to the metronoming
of wind battering
billboards. Bass *low*

sibilant hiss of dull yellow
rain meeting streetlight,
joining the counterpoint,
dissonance, castanets
or maybe

that's just the cockroaches,
dirty legs skittering over
tin foil dance floor. The
baby is crying.

Listen.

Gratitude

This book and most of the poems I've ever written exist because of people who have touched my life, in ways powerful and resonant. I want to take a moment to thank some of them for existing and for inspiring me to keep seeking beauty in all things.

My gratitude first to Katrina K Guarascio, who is not only an amazing Editor and Publisher, but a wonderful co-conspirator and tour mate! You have been one of my truest friends for a very long time and your honesty about both the writing and life out loud have been nothing short of amazing!

I also want to thank my other best friend and favorite light bearing poet, Jessica Helen Lopez. The fearlessness of your words and your life inspire me constantly to write more, better, and dig deeper. Your friendship over the years has been a salve and a treasure.

Both of you mean the world to me, which is why I don't tell you which poems are about you. Just kidding.

And always, always my thanks and endless love to my children, who are the inspiration for my breath, which results in these words being born so often. You are the single brightest collection of lights any sky has ever known and it is not a reflection, it is you. You are the source. I love you endlessly and am proud to be your papa.

Many thanks to the ABQ slams community where I cut my teeth and learned to stand up among the giants, whether I reached their measure or not. Thank you for supporting me and letting me learn from you all.

To all of the editors, publishers, poets and venue owners out there who have invited me to read and perform, thank you. And to all of the social justice agencies and organizations I have had the pleasure of working with to create a lasting change, thank you for your inspiration and light. The change is here. Now let us guide it safely in positive directions.

Thank you reader, for being so kind and trusting to read my words and spend time with them. As a fan of the sublime, I seek beauty in dark corners and I hope you find it there in these poems.

About the Author

A performance poet since 2006, Zachary Kluckman is a two-time member of the Albuquerque national poetry slam team, a Pushcart Prize nominee, and recipient of the Red Mountain Press National Poetry Prize.

His work appears in print globally in numerous anthologies and publications including the New York Quarterly, Cutthroat, Red Fez and more. Featured on over 500 radio stations, with appearances on many of the nation's most notorious stages, he is an accomplished spoken word artist, as well as the Spoken Word Editor for the Pedestal.

An activist, youth advocate and organizer, he has been recognized twice for making world history as the creator of the world's only Slam Poet Laureate Program and an organizer for the 100 Thousand Poets for Change program, the largest poetry reading in history.

As a youth advocate, Kluckman donates hundreds of hours a year to working with and empowering the youth. His first full length collection, Animals in our Flesh, has received warm reviews from Jimmy Santiago Baca among others.

Acknowledgements

The author would like to gratefully acknowledge the Editors and Publishers of the following journals, who were kind enough to publish some of these poems before:

- Gesture Literary Journal
- The Malpais Review
- Red Fez
- Mad Hatter
- Poetry Nook
- The New York Quarterly
- Memoir (and)

Some of these poems previously appeared in the chapbook, *The Curious Circus*, published by UNCOLA Press 2013 and *Animals In Our Flesh*, Red Mountain Press 2012.

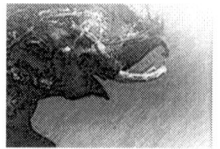

Copyright © 2014 Swimming with Elephants Publications

52453811R00061

Made in the USA
Columbia, SC
04 March 2019